A Child's Christmas ABC Book

A Child's Christmas ABC Book

Angels in the Air Arrayed

Paul Thigpen   Illustrated by John Folley

Copyright © 2020 Paul Thigpen.

All rights reserved. With the exception of short excerpts used in critical review, no part of this work may be reproduced, transmitted, or stored in any form whatsoever without the prior written permission of the publisher.

Illustrations by John Folley.

Graphic design by Caroline Green.

ISBN: 978-1-5051-1631-1

Published in the United States by
TAN Books
P. O. Box 410487
Charlotte, NC 28241
www.TANBooks.com

Printed and bound in the United States of America

For all my spiritual
sons and daughters,
with much love
and many prayers.

-Paul Thigpen

To my beautiful wife,
Deirdre, without whom
this book would have
never been possible.

-John Folley

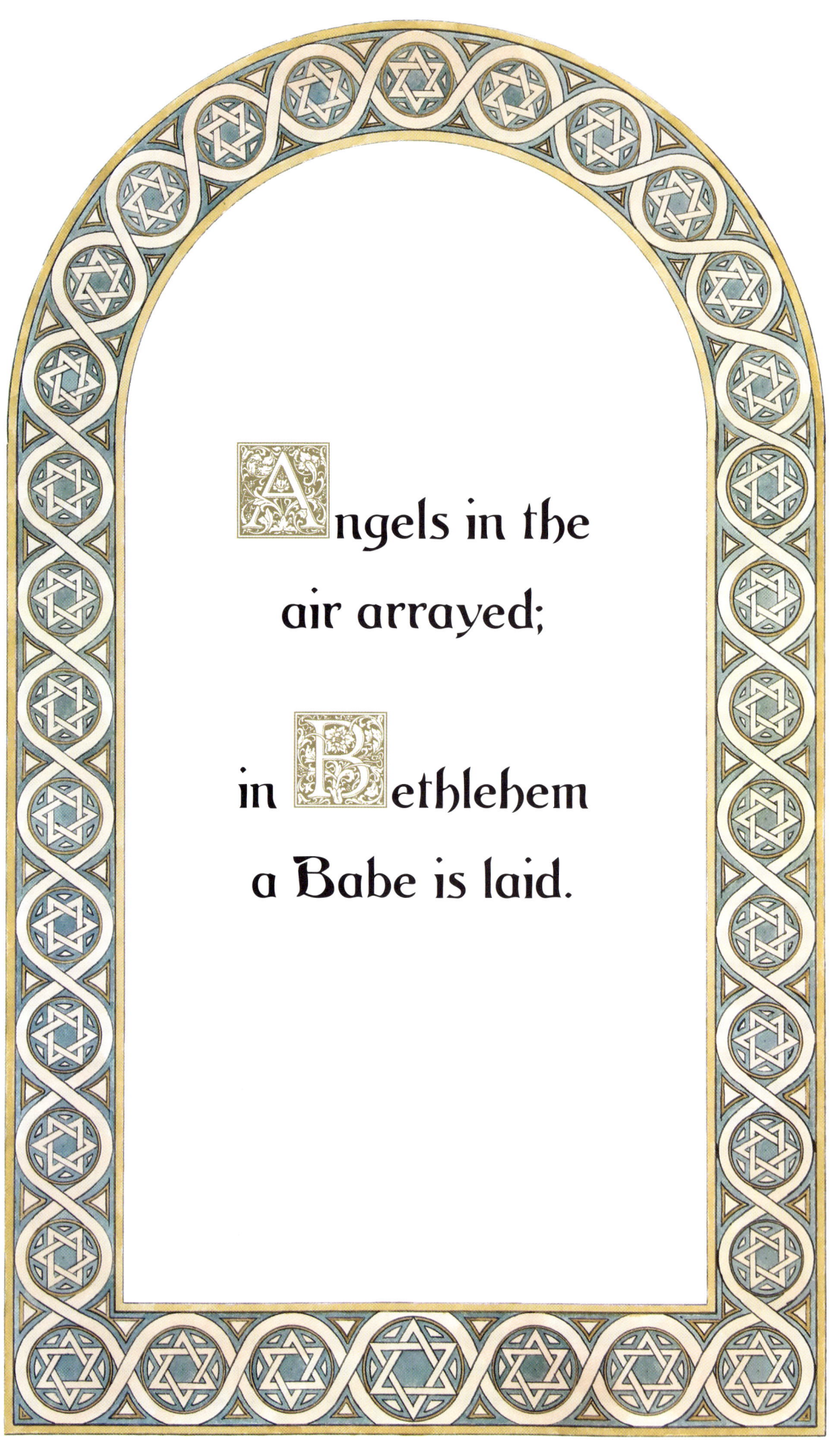

Angels in the air arrayed;

in Bethlehem a Babe is laid.

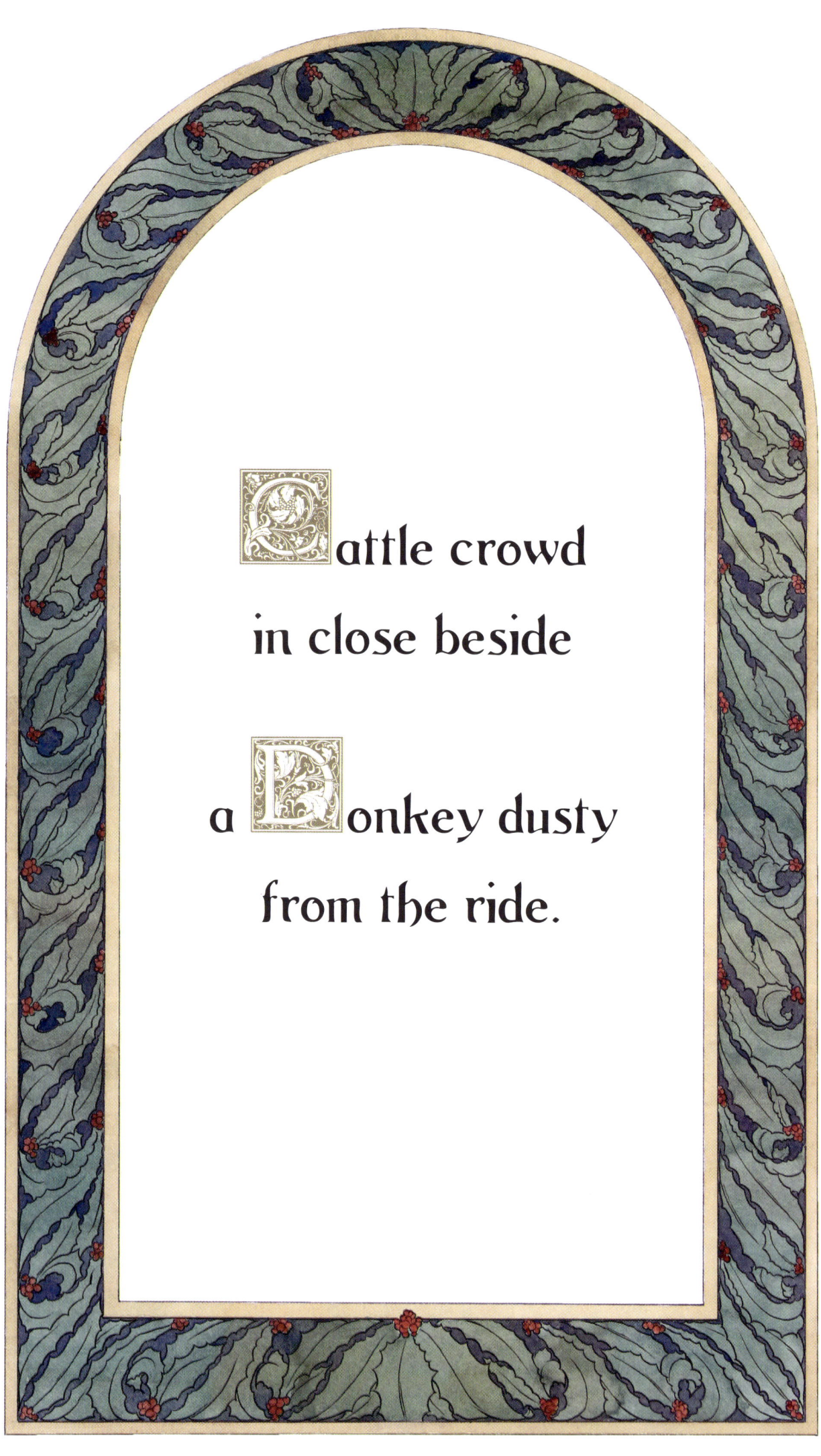

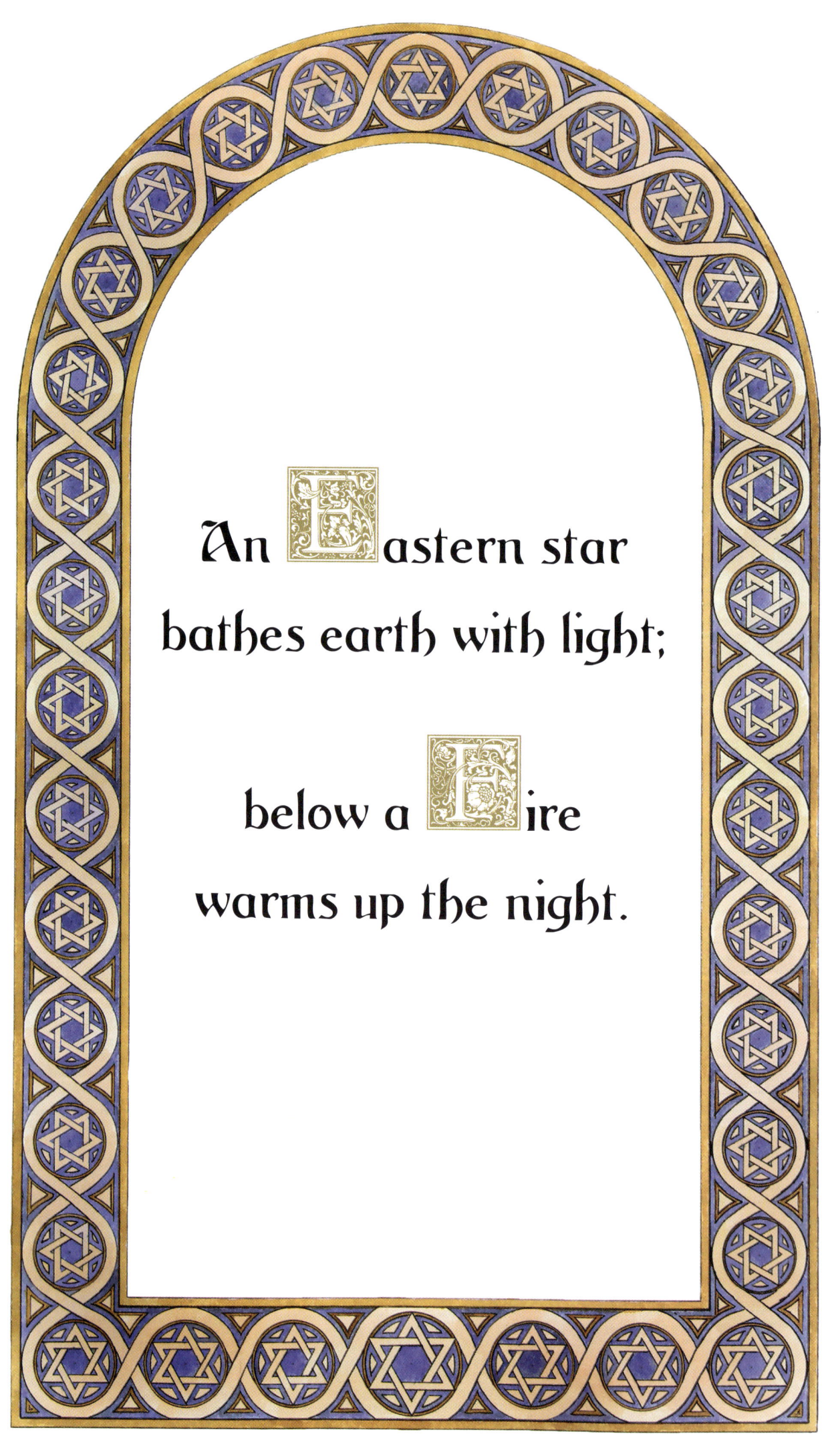

An Eastern star bathes earth with light;

below a Fire warms up the night.

God gives His Gift, the Lord of grace,

with Hay a halo 'round His face.

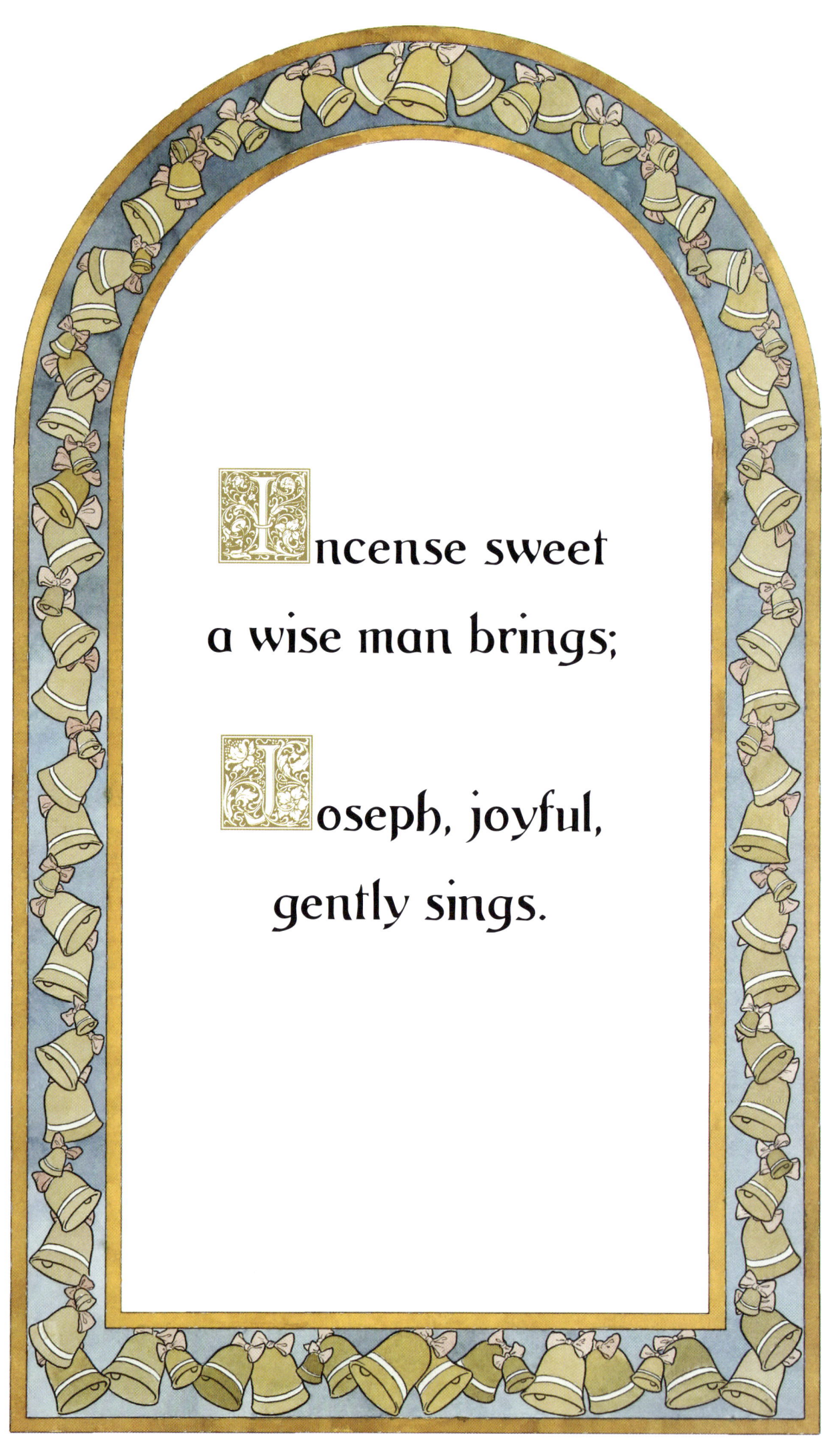

Incense sweet
a wise man brings;

Joseph, joyful,
gently sings.

Kings before this
King bow down

while little Lambs
leap all around.

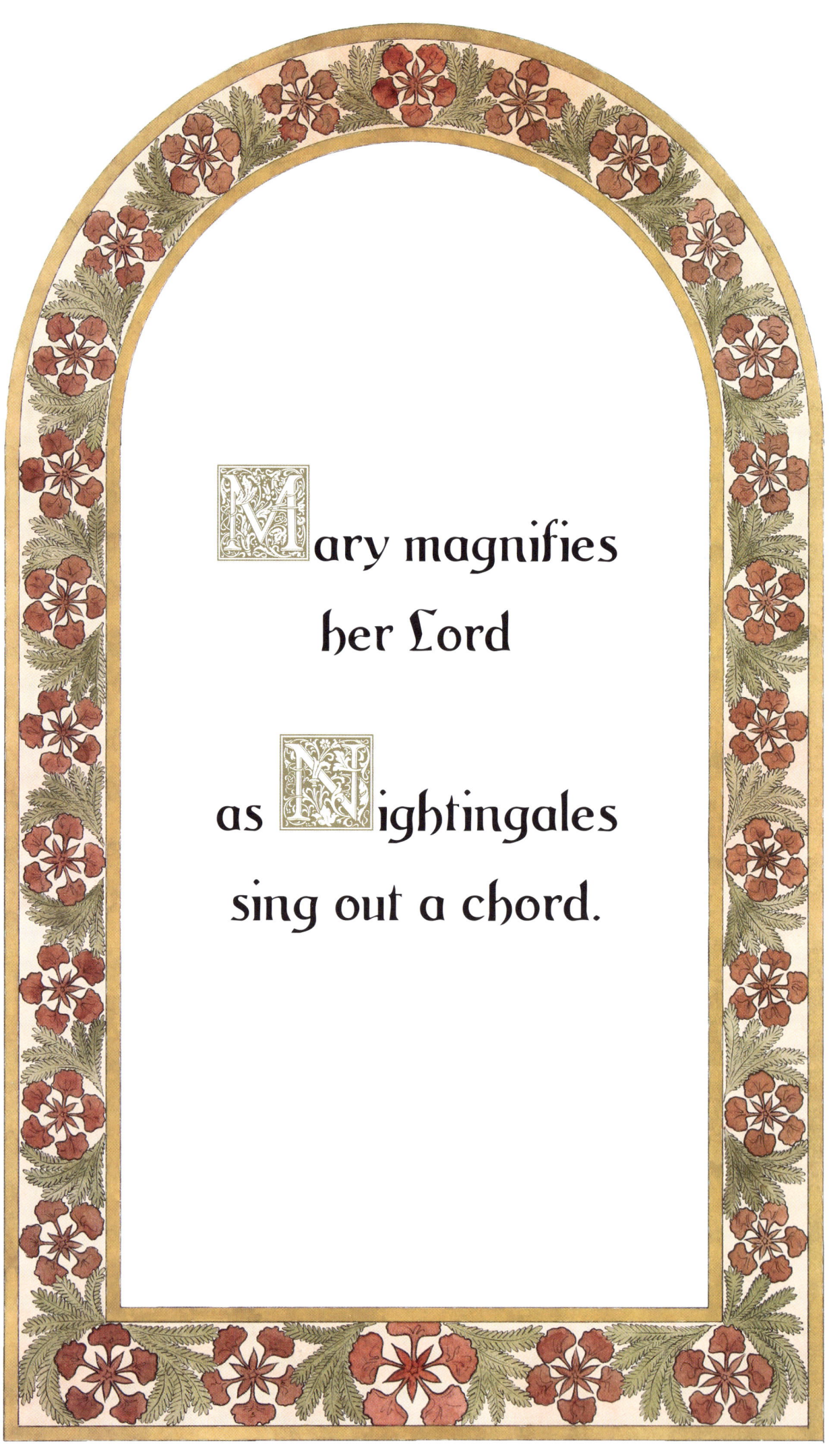

Mary magnifies her Lord

as Nightingales sing out a chord.

Olive trees chant in the wind:

"Peace on earth, good will to men!"

Quarreling shepherds
silent fall as

Royal heralds
sound a call:

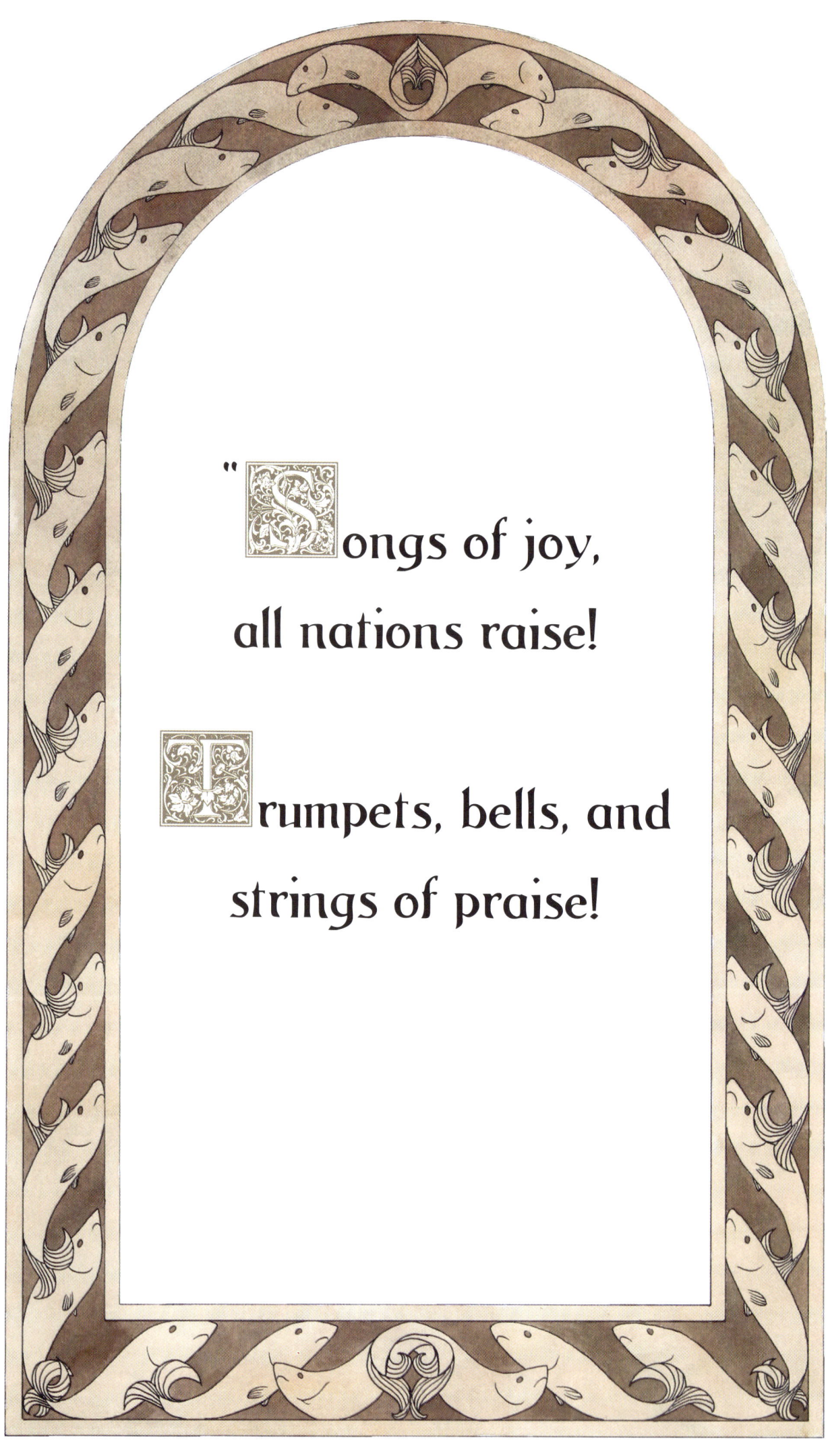

"Songs of joy, all nations raise!

Trumpets, bells, and strings of praise!

The Universe in harmony:

Valleys, mountains, sky and sea!

Wake and sing,
the good news share

Glad eXultation
everywhere!

Young Lord Jesus, we adore,

Zion's King forevermore!"

𝔓aul 𝔗higpen, 𝔓h𝔇, is the author of fifty-five books. His five books for children were first written for his own little ones and are now enjoyed by his grandchildren and godchildren as well.

John Folley is an independent artist and illustrator trained in the Boston School Tradition. John formerly taught at the Heights School in Potomac, Maryland, as head of their Art Department and is a currently Visiting Fellow and Art Guild Master at the Thomas More College of Liberal Arts in Merrimack, New Hampshire. John has done illustration work for books, magazines, and businesses and his figurative fine art work includes portraits, still life, illuminations, and landscape paintings in homes, businesses, and churches across the United States. His studio is on the historic town green in Lancaster, Massachusetts, where he also resides with his wife, Deirdre, and their four young children. John advocates for a revival of true standards for beauty in Art at www.johnfolley.com.